Aspects of the New Ri

Aspects of the New Right-Wing Extremism

Theodor W. Adorno

With an Afterword by Volker Weiss

Translated by Wieland Hoban

polity

Originally published in German as *Aspekte des neuen Rechtsradikalismus* © Suhrkamp Verlag Berlin, 2019. All rights reserved by and controlled through Suhrkamp Verlag Berlin.

This edition © Polity Press, 2020

Polity Press
65 Bridge Street
Cambridge CB2 1UR, UK

Polity Press
101 Station Landing
Suite 300
Medford, MA 02155, USA

ISBN-13: 978-1-5095-4144-7
ISBN-13: 978-1-5095-4145-4 (pb)

A catalogue record for this book is available from the British Library.

Typeset in 12.5 on 15 pt Adobe Garamond by Servis Filmsetting Ltd, Stockport, Cheshire
Printed and bound in Great Britain by TJ Books Limited.

The publisher has used its best endeavours to ensure that the URLs for external websites referred to in this book are correct and active at the time of going to press. However, the publisher has no responsibility for the websites and can make no guarantee that a site will remain live or that the content is or will remain appropriate.

Every effort has been made to trace all copyright holders, but if any have been overlooked the publisher will be pleased to include any necessary credits in any subsequent reprint or edition.

For further information on Polity, visit our website: politybooks.com

Contents

Aspects of the New Right-Wing Extremism

So, ladies and gentlemen,

I will not attempt to present a theory of right-wing extremism with any claim to comprehensiveness but, rather, I will highlight with some informal observations a few things of which you may not all be aware. It is thus not my intention to invalidate other theoretical interpretations, simply to add a little to what is generally thought and known about these matters.

In 1959 I gave a lecture entitled 'The Meaning of Working through the Past', in which I developed the thesis that the reason for right-wing extremism, or the potential for such a right-wing extremism, which was not yet truly visible at the time, is that the social conditions for fascism continue to exist. So I will work on the assumption, ladies and gentlemen, that, despite the collapse of fascism itself, the conditions for fascist movements are still socially, if not politically, present. Here I am thinking especially of the still prevailing tendency towards concentration of capital, which one can calculate away with all manner of statistical arts but which cannot seriously be doubted. At the same time, this tendency towards concentration still creates the possibility of constantly downgrading strata of society that were clearly bourgeois in terms of their subjective class consciousness and want to cling to, and possibly reinforce, their privileges and social status. These groups still tend towards a hatred of socialism, or what they call socialism; that is, they lay the blame for their own potential downgrading not on the apparatus that causes it, but on those who were critical towards the system in which they once had a status, at least in a traditional sense. Whether they are still critical and have the same practices today is another matter.

Now, the transition to socialism or, more modestly put, even just to socialist organizations has always been very difficult for these groups, and today, at least in Germany – and naturally my experiences relate primarily to Germany – it is even harder than it used to be. This is mostly because the SPD, the German social democratic party, is identified with a Keynesianism, a Keynesian liberalism that, on the one hand, deflects the potential for a change in social structures that was part of classical Marxian theory and, on the other hand, increases the threat of impoverishment, at least as a final consequence, for the social strata to which I referred. Let me remind you of the simple fact of the creeping, yet very noticeable inflation, which is a consequence precisely of Keynesian expansionism. Let me also recall a thesis that I developed in that study eight years ago, and which has meanwhile begun to gain relevance considerably, namely that, despite full employment and all such symptoms of prosperity, the spectre of technological unemployment continues to haunt society to such a degree that in the age of automation, which is less advanced in Central Europe but will undoubtedly catch up, even the people who stand within the production process already feel potentially superfluous – I put this very starkly – they really feel potentially unemployed. In addition there is the fear of the East, both because of the lower standard of living there and because of the lack of freedom, which is experienced in very direct and real terms by the people, the masses too, and also, at least until recently, the feeling of a foreign threat.

We must now remind ourselves of the remarkable situation that currently prevails with regard to the problem of nationalism in the age of the great power blocs. For, within these blocs, nationalism lives on as an organ of collective interest groups within the large-scale groups under discussion. It is beyond doubt that, in both socio-psychological and real terms, there is a very widespread fear of being absorbed by these blocs and, in the process, being severely impaired in one's material existence. Thus, when it comes to the potential of right-wing extremism in agriculture, there is no doubt an extremely great fear of the EEC and the consequences of the EEC for the agricultural market.

At the same time, however – and this touches on the antagonistic character of the new nationalism, or right-wing extremism – there is something fictitious about it if one looks at the grouping of the world of today into these few oversized blocs, where the individual nations and states really play only a secondary part. No one really believes in that any more. The individual nation's freedom of movement is heavily restricted by its integration into the large power blocs. One should not, however, draw the primitive conclusion from this that, because it is now obsolete, nationalism no longer plays a significant role; on the contrary, it is very often the case that convictions and ideologies take on their demonic, their genuinely destructive character precisely when the objective situation has deprived them of substance. The witch trials, after all, took place not at the height of Thomism but during the Counter-Reformation, and something similar is probably the case with, if I may term it thus, the 'pathic' nationalism of today. This aspect of selling something to people in which they themselves do not entirely believe was, incidentally, already evident in Hitler's day. And this fluctuation, this ambivalence between an overwrought nationalism and the doubt about it, which has to be covered up so that one can convince oneself and others, so to speak – this could already be observed back then.

Now, let me draw a few initial conclusions from these rather basic theses. For I think that what I have told you – that it is essentially about a fear of the consequences of overall social developments

– explains what has been observed everywhere by polling institutes and was also confirmed by our own work, namely that the adherents of old and new fascism can be found in all areas of today's society. I think the very widespread belief that all these movements are a specifically petty bourgeois phenomenon, as observed recently in French Poujadism, is accurate in terms of their social character, shall we say, but that this thesis is inaccurate when it comes to their distribution, even though certain petty bourgeois groups are undoubtedly susceptible, especially small merchants who are directly threatened by the concentration of the retail sector in department stores and similar institutions. Aside from them, another major group is the farmers, who are in a constant crisis, and I would think that, until the agricultural problem is solved in a radical way, one that is not artificial and based on subsidy and problematic in itself, until a sensible and rational collectivization of agriculture is achieved, this virulent breeding-ground will remain fertile.

Beyond this, however, these movements also show something like an increasing discrepancy between provincial and urban areas. Specific groups, such as the small winery owners in the

German Palatinate region, also seem especially susceptible. As far as the industrial backing of these movements is concerned, we do not yet have genuinely concrete evidence of this. One must be very careful in all these matters not to think too schematically, for example by applying the schema of industry pushing fascism – one must not operate carelessly with such models. One must also bear in mind that fascism, whose apparatus always has a tendency to take on a life of its own in relation to the central economic interests, is not actually convenient for big industry, and that fascism was adopted in Germany as a last resort, at the moment of an extremely severe economic crisis that evidently left the Ruhr industry, which had gone bankrupt, with no alternative.

Of course there are old Nazi cadres. But here too, I would say – based merely on observations that have been made in empirical social research – that one should not think one is dealing simply with the so-called incorrigibles, the type of people we merely shrug our shoulders about. Young followers are undoubtedly being attracted too, especially the kind who experienced the collapse in 1945 as fifteen-year-olds, shall we say, and developed this extremely strong feeling that 'Germany has to be on top again.'

Perhaps I can say from a socio-psychological perspective, though goodness knows I do not consider these to be primarily psychological matters, that in 1945 there was no true panic, no true breakdown of identification with the regime and discipline as took place in Italy, but that it remained coherent to the end. Identification with the system was never really radically destroyed in Germany, and this is naturally one of the possibilities: that the groups I am referring to can take this up again.

One very often hears, especially when it comes to such categories as the 'eternally incorrigible' and similar consolatory phrases, the claim that there is a residue of incorrigibles or fools, a so-called lunatic fringe, as they term it in America, in every democracy. And then there is a certain quietist bourgeois comfort in reciting that to oneself. I think the only response to this is that, yes, something like this can be observed to a varying degree in every so-called democracy in the world, but only as an expression that, in terms of its content, its socio-economic content, democracy has not yet become truly and fully concrete anywhere but is still formal. In that sense, one might refer to the fascist movements as the wounds, the scars of a democracy that, to this day, has not yet lived up to its own concept.

Furthermore, to correct certain clichéd notions about these matters, I would also say that the relationship between these movements and the economy is a structural relationship, that it lies in that tendency towards concentration and immiseration, but that one should not imagine it as a short-term phenomenon, and that, if one simply equates right-wing extremism with economic developments, one can arrive at very wrong conclusions. Thus the successes of the NPD[1] in Germany were already somewhat alarming before the economic setback, and in a sense anticipated it – or, if you will, discounted it. One might say that they forestalled a fear and terror that only subsequently became truly explicit.

I think this reference to anticipating terror touches on something very central that, as far as I can see, is given far too little attention in the usual views about right-wing extremism, namely the very complex and difficult relationship with the feeling of social catastrophe that prevails here. One might speak of a distortion of Marx's theory

of collapse that takes place in this very crip-
pled and false consciousness. On the one hand,
on the rational side of things, they ask, 'What
will happen if there is a big crisis?' – and that is
where these movements are attractive. On the
other hand, they also have something in common
with the type of manipulated astrology one finds
today, which I consider an extremely important and typical socio-psychological symptom,
because, in a sense, they want the catastrophe,
they feed off apocalyptic fantasies of the kind
that, as it happens, could also be found among
the Nazi leadership, as documents show.

If I had to speak psychoanalytically, I would
say that, of the forces mobilized here, the appeal
to the unconscious desire for disaster, for catastrophe, is by no means the least significant in
these movements. But I would add – and I am
speaking especially to those of you who are
rightly sceptical about any merely psychological
interpretation of social and political phenomena
– that this behaviour is by no means purely psy-
chologically motivated; it also has an objective
basis. Someone who is unable to see anything
ahead of them and does not want the social foun-
dation to change really has no alternative but,

like Richard Wagner's Wotan, to say, 'Do you know what Wotan wants? The end.' This person, from the perspective of their own social situation, longs for demise – though not the demise of their own group, as far as possible, the demise of all.

If I could say one more thing about the specifically German aspect of the rise of the NPD, the function of the concept of organization surely plays a very important part here. For the first time, alone by adapting its name to those of the other parties, the NPD carried out something like an organizational mass appeal without the sectarian whiff that clung to the NPD's extremist forerunners, the Socialist Reich Party and the rest of them. What works in Germany – and this seems to be a specifically German element that cannot automatically be transferred to Austria – is something tightly and centrally organized, whereas anything that gives even remotely the impression of a sect, that does not present itself from the start as having all manner of support, is viewed with suspicion in Germany and cannot have any mass appeal. It is one of the basic tenets of German ideology that there must be no loners. It is no coincidence that people repeatedly quoted Hindenburg as saying, 'Be united,

united, united!'; and the fight against the 'party nuisance' – the idea that political compromise per se is already something degenerate – this is such a deep-seated belief in the German bourgeoisie that to this day, even with the change of political form, little about this ideology has changed.

So people want to have support behind them, and that explains the major role of the so-called bandwagon effect, as the Americans term it, namely that these movements always act as if they have already had great successes and attract people through the pretence that they offer guarantees for the future and have all manner of backing. No doubt a further element in this unity complex is the fact that, in Germany, the nation-state is something that was realized only very belatedly, compared above all to England and France. And the people in Germany seem to live in perpetual fear for their national identity, a fear that clearly contributes to an overvaluation of national consciousness. This would also explain the panic that seizes Germans at the thought of division.

One should not underestimate these movements on account of their low intellectual level and lack of theory. I think it would show a very weak political eye if one concluded from this that they are unsuccessful. Rather, what characterizes these movements is an extraordinary perfection of certain methods, first of all of propagandist methods in the broadest sense, combined with the blindness, indeed abstruseness, of the aims they pursue. And I think that precisely this constellation of rational means and irrational ends, if I can put it in such a simplified form, in a sense corresponds to the overall tendency of civilization, which leads to such a perfection of techniques and means while the overall social purpose falls by the wayside. The ingenuity of the propaganda used by these parties and movements is that it balances out the difference, the unquestionable difference between the real interests and the fraudulent aims they espouse. It is the very substance of the matter, just as it was with the Nazis. When the means increasingly become substitutes for aims, one can almost say that, in these extreme right-wing movements, propaganda actually constitutes the substance of politics. And it is no coincidence that the so-called leaders of German National Socialism, the likes of Hitler and Goebbels, were first and foremost propagandists, and that their productivity and imagination went into propaganda.

I do not, incidentally, think one should exaggerate the conflicts in the controlling body of the German NPD. If my impression is correct, the so-called hard or radical wing has triumphed. Here we should recall the former relationship between the Nazi Party and Hugenberg's German Nationalists. They still have no mass base, and the mass base seems to go hand in hand with that element of disaster politics, of self-exaggeration, if you like, of that element of delusion.

In this context it is also interesting, and should be noted by political scientists and especially by the actual politicians who analyse these things, that such structures, despite the disasters, have a peculiar constancy; that, despite the great catastrophe, something like the fact that the German Nationalists were defeated in the power struggle with the National Socialists seems to be repeating itself in the power struggles within the NPD.

Political groupings outlast systems and disasters. In Germany, for example, old National Socialist centres like northern Hesse, where there was already a wild anti-Semitic movement in the 1880s, and northern Bavaria seem to be especially susceptible. Groups that define themselves almost automatically in opposition to both conservatism and the left, because of this double front, tend towards right-wing extremism, and I should imagine that you have observed this structure in Austria too. Of course, one should not fail to mention all the manipulation and coercion of these movements, the fact that they are somewhat akin to the ghost of a ghost. It would be wrong, and it would be hysterical, if one imagined these things in Germany today as a form of spontaneous mass movement. But certainly such a movement can develop if the potential offered by the objective conditions is seized and exploited in escalating situations. And in this case it is no doubt true that the extremist groups gain the upper hand through a dynamic that repeatedly shows itself in these situations. We have not reached that point yet, but, on the other hand, one should not take the numbers arrived at by the pollsters – which are, incidentally, far from insignificant – as invariants. The fact that people do not fully believe in the cause does not make things any better. This does offer a possibility to develop a defence – one can certainly use these contradictions, and this only partial belief, to combat such tendencies – but herein also lies the possibility, the potential of these movements themselves: they grow into delusional systems, and there can no longer be any doubt that so-called mass movements of a fascist nature have a very deep structural connection to delusional systems. One important factor here is the anthropological type, which I referred to in *The Authoritarian Personality* as the 'manipulative type' – at a time, incidentally, when all the material about the likes of Himmler, Höss or Eichmann had not yet even come to light, working purely with the material that we had gathered in our empirical social research. So these are people who are simultaneously cold, without relationships, strictly technological in their mindset – but also insane in a certain sense, as Himmler was to a prototypical degree. And this strange unity of a delusional system and technological perfection, this seems to be on the rise and once again playing a decisive part in these movements.

On the other hand, ladies and gentlemen, one must naturally place great emphasis on the differences compared to the Weimar period if one is to avoid thinking in schematic analogies again. The first thing to mention is the after-effect of defeat. This defeat, however, was covered up by the period of prosperity. And this is where a decisive opposition to these things can begin. One should not operate primarily with ethical appeals, with appeals to humanity, for the word 'humanity' itself, and everything associated with it, sends the people in question into a rage; they see it as fear and weakness – just as, in particular incidents I know about, the mention of Auschwitz led to calls of 'Hooray for Auschwitz' and the mere mention of Jewish names already caused laughter.

The only thing – I will jump to this now, because I think it is one of the most crucial aspects of how to resist this movement – the only thing that really strikes me as effective is to warn the potential followers of right-wing extremism about its own consequences, to convey to them that this politics will inevitably lead its own followers to their doom too, and that this doom was part of it from the outset, just as Hitler started saying, at an early stage, 'Then I'd rather put a bullet in my head', and then repeated the claim at every opportunity. So if one is serious about opposing these things, one must refer to the central interests of those who are targeted by the propaganda. This applies especially to young people, whom one must warn about every kind of drill, about the restriction of their privacy and their lifestyle.

And one must warn them about the cult of a so-called order that does not answer to reason, especially the concept of discipline, which is presented as an end in itself, without anyone asking 'Discipline for what?' And obviously the fetishization of everything military expressed in such lovely phrases as 'soldierly man' [*der soldatische Mensch*] belongs in this context.

A further difference one must keep in mind is that of political intertwinement. Today, Germany is not a political subject in anything like the way it was in the Weimar period. There is even a risk that precisely this movement might remove Germany from world politics, from the tendency of world politics as such, and completely provincialize it. On the one hand, this places far greater real-world restrictions on such a politics, unless other and far more powerful countries also experience a triumph of right-wing extremism. On the other hand, that very fact stirs up anger. And this anger is likely to be vented especially in what one calls the 'cultural sector'. I would therefore argue – to say nothing about the direct interests that a cultured person has in these matters – that, from the political perspective too, the symptoms of reactionary culture and forced provincialization must be observed with particular vigilance, because this – simply because these movements have no room for manoeuvre in foreign policy terms – is the area in which they can rage most and will surely try and try even more to rage. There is a whole array of designated enemies. One of these is the imago of the communist. In the Weimar Republic, the Communist Party was very strong in numbers, and there was at least a certain plausibility in the political rivalry between the Nazis and the communists, although the deployment of the Reichswehr undoubtedly inflated the true significance of what was called the 'communist threat'. Today there is no longer a communist party in Germany, and this has really given communism a sort of mythical character – that is, it has become completely abstract; and this peculiar abstractness means that anything that somehow does not fit is subsumed under this all-purpose term 'communism' and opposed as something communist. The notorious 'Congo Müller', for example, a man who lived in Germany, a German who had evidently played an especially gruesome part among the mercenaries in the Congo, declared that, wherever in the world communism needed to be opposed, he would immediately join the fight, because this was in keeping with democracy.

Now, this is divorced from any knowledge about the matter. Communism has been reduced to a bugbear. One factor in this – as another bugbear – is the concept of materialism, though people confuse, in a very primitive fashion, the materialism of the pursuit of profit and the interest in material advantages with the materialist theory of history, thus behaving as if those who want to change this system were nothing but vulgar materialists who simply want more.

Incidentally, I consider it one of the more peculiar divisions that still exist within class consciousness – and we have quite concrete material on this – that those who identify with bourgeois class consciousness in the broadest sense consider themselves idealists, whereas the workers, who are still the ones who have to foot the bill, show a certain kind of scepticism that has little to do with the theory but stands in extremely sharp opposition to the ideological nature of that so-called idealism, which is a vulgar idealism – for there is not only vulgar materialism but also vulgar idealism.

Then another *bête noire*, of course – as long as one cannot be openly anti-Semitic and as long as one cannot murder the Jews, because that has already happened – consists of the intellectuals, who are especially hated. The phrase 'left-wing intellectual' is another one of these bugbears. It appeals first of all to the German distrust towards anyone who does not hold some office, some established position, who is viewed as a kind of vagrant in life, an 'air person', as one used to call it in Poland. According to this ideology, whoever does not participate in the division of labour, whoever is not bound by their profession to a particular position and thus also to quite particular ideas, but has instead preserved their freedom of spirit, this person is a kind of rascal who needs to be brought into line. The age-old resentment of the manual labourer towards intellectual work also plays a part here, of course, but it has been shifted and become entirely unrecognizable to itself.

Because these movements, which, as I say, are essentially no more than techniques of power and by no means based on any developed theory – because they are helpless in the face of the spirit, they attack the bearers of spirit. As Valéry, who can hardly be accused of being left-wing, so eloquently put it: 'If someone is cleverer than oneself, he is a sophist.' Here the separation of so-called rationality and so-called feeling is reified. In this context I cannot refrain from pointing out that the observations I made in *The Jargon of Authenticity* about the role of the concept of the existential and existence in existential philosophy, at least in its Central European manifestations, have been confirmed. In a recent polemic against a professor who does not suit their agenda, for example, the right-wing extremists said, 'We will not have any discussions with her; it is a matter of existential opposites.' So you can see from this how directly the concept of the existential is placed in the service of irrationalism, of the rejection of rational argumentation, of discursive thought as such. And I do think the toxic climate of existential philosophy that prevails in German-language thought bears a considerable share of the blame for the preparation of anti-intellectualism among intellectuals.

Obviously, in spite of everything, anti-Semitism continues to be a 'plank of the platform'. It outlived the Jews, one might say, and that is the source of its own ghostly nature. In particular, feelings of guilt are fended off by rationalization: 'There must be something in it, otherwise they wouldn't have killed them.' Now, of course, there has been official legislation to make these things taboo. But even the taboo about mentioning the Jews becomes a means of anti-Semitic incitement, with a wink and a nudge: 'We're not allowed to say it, but we understand each other. We all know what we mean.' And, in this technique of allusion, the mere mention of a Jewish name is already sufficient to create certain effects.

One technique in the new manipulation of anti-Semitism to which I would like to draw your attention, so that you can perhaps study it a little more closely and resist it, is cumulative effect. A publication like the *Soldaten-Zeitung*, that is, the *National-Zeitung*, has developed a remarkable virtuosity in never writing anything in one issue that is extreme enough to warrant intervention based on the current, quite firm laws against anti-Semitism or neo-Nazism. On the other hand, if one looks at a number of issues in succession, one must truly be stricken with the spirit of formalism not to see what they mean. And this danger, this form of allusion that has been elevated to a sophisticated technique, is one of those things that should not only be studied closely and pin-pointed; one should surely also try to find legal means by which a democratic state would be able to intervene.

So, as far as this ideology goes, the law prevents it from expressing itself fully. One might say that all ideological expressions of right-wing extremism are characterized by a constant conflict between not being allowed to say something and those things that, as one agitator recently described it, are intended to bring audiences to boiling point – and it did not succeed in this, you will be reassured to know. This conflict is not only external, however, for the requirement to adapt to democratic rules also leads to a certain change in behaviour, and in this sense there is an element – how shall I put it? – an element of inner division that these movements tend to have in their revenant stage. Openly anti-democratic aspects are removed. On the contrary: they constantly invoke true democracy and accuse the others of being anti-democratic. And there is a certain contradiction in the concessions to democratic rules, as the demagogic element can no longer be indulged in so unreservedly. Recall the problem of intra-party democracy, for example, which is guaranteed by the German constitution. Where intra-party democracy is violated, a party risks being banned. If it is maintained, however, this political form is essentially irreconcilable with what is being espoused. This is another aspect that should be taken into account in strategies for opposition.

In its content, of course, this ideology, in so far as it is an independent, fully developed ideology – and I consider the ideological component entirely secondary to the political will to have one's turn – is essentially based on Nazi ideology. When one reads the documents, it is amazing how little in the way of new elements has been added to the old repertoire, how secondary and rehashed it is. At most, they have tried to usurp European integration, to speak of a 'European nation', but this has evidently proved highly unappealing for reasons of nationalism, which is an attempt to assert oneself in the midst of integration and is a stronger force. So here we find another form of contradiction.

Something that plays a very important part in the ideology – and here I am genuinely referring to a scientific problem, albeit a problem to which I cannot presume to offer you any real solution – is anti-Americanism, which was pre-figured in the talk of 'plutocratic' nations and such things in the Nazi period. In keeping with this anti-Americanism, it attempts to usurp the idea of Europe as a 'third power'. It is difficult to say what is behind anti-Americanism. It probably stems partly from something that is genuinely felt, namely that, even under formal democracy, people feel deprived of the full freedom of political choice by the system of blocs – and this is not only a feeling. I would like to point out here – perhaps I can say this in passing – that by no means all elements of this ideology are simply untrue, but that true elements are also used in the service of an untrue ideology, and that the art of opposing this lies substantially in picking out the abuse of truth for untruth and resisting it. The most important technique whereby the truth is placed in the service of untruth is that true or accurate observations are taken out of their context, isolated, for example, by saying, 'Life under Hitler was fine until he started that stupid war', without seeing that the entire boom between '33 and '39 was only possible because of the hectic war economy, by the preparations for war. And there are a hundred similar things.

So this follows on from the whole complex around autonomy, which is after all the aim of democracy but is not fully realized in the prevailing system. If I am not mistaken, some of the most effective slogans of neo-fascism use phrases like 'Now one can choose again.'[2] Or that – in a variation on a slogan by Goebbels, with his reference to the 'system parties' – they speak of the 'licence parties' – that is, the parties that were licensed by the former occupying powers. And this was incredibly effective, because people had the feeling that now, with this movement that seeks precisely to abolish freedom, they are regaining their freedom, their freedom of decision and spontaneity. I think it would be important in particular to examine very closely this motive, which is very much interwoven with that of anti-Americanism.

A fundamental aspect of this ideology is its fragmentary nature. Many 'planks' such as the eastward expansion, imperialism in the true sense, have fallen away willy-nilly. The prospect of 'tomorrow the whole world' is completely absent, which gives the whole thing rather a lack of impetus and makes it rely more on desperation than was subliminally the case in National

Socialism. But let me say again that there was never a truly, fully developed theory in fascism; it was always implied that what mattered was power, conceptless praxis and, ultimately, unconditional domination, and that spirit of the kind that expresses itself in theory was secondary by comparison. And that in turn gave these movements an ideological flexibility, of course, that can be observed so widely. This is also part of the Zeitgeist: the predominance of a conceptless praxis, which also has consequences for propaganda.

Let me close with some reflections on propaganda, which, as I hinted earlier, I really consider the centre, even the matter itself in a certain sense. This propaganda is less concerned with the dissemination of an ideology which, as I told you, is too thin to draw in the masses. So propaganda here is primarily a technique of mass psychology. It is based on the model of the authority-bound personality, in the same way today as in the time of Hitler or in the movements of the 'lunatic fringe' in America or anywhere else. The unity lies in this appeal to the authority-bound personality. One hears time and again that these movements all promise something, and that is true as a characteristic of the lack of theory. But it is false in the sense that there is a very specific, emphatic unity in this appeal to the authority-bound character. You will never find a single utterance that does not correspond to the schema of the authority-bound personality. And if one uncovers this structure of the appeal to the authority-bound personality, this truly sends the right-wing extremists into a rage, and I think this constitutes a degree of proof that one has struck a sore point in this structure. So the unconscious tendencies that feed the authority-bound personality are not brought to light by this propaganda; on the contrary, they are forced even deeper into the unconscious; they are kept artificially unconscious. Consider the excessive significance of so-called symbols that characterizes all these movements.

But if one brings these things up, people suddenly become very scientific; they explain that the evidence of the authority-bound personality, that this cannot be proved statistically with the necessary exactitude, and so on and so forth, and they use the methods of a perverted positivism to inhibit experience, living experience. This, incidentally, is the point at which the problems

I had the privilege of speaking to you about last night[3] directly converge with those I am discussing today.

Psychoanalysis is hated most of all, of course, along with anti-intellectualism, the fear that the unconscious will become conscious, and the authoritarian character, which form a kind of syndrome together. This propaganda technique rests on both certain formal traits and varyingly isolated individual topics. It has long been my conviction – and Horkheimer and I have already worked on this particular problem in America – that there are a relatively small number of recurring, standardized and completely objectified tricks that are very poor and thin in themselves yet, by being constantly repeated, gain a certain propagandist value for these movements.

On the formal side of things, I would first like to draw your attention to something one must take into account in one's opposition, and it is not such an easy matter. It is the appeal to concretism, as I call it. The approach – and this is evidently cultivated especially by the NPD in Germany – is always to work with an accumulation of data, especially numbers, to which one cannot usually respond, with an undertone like this: 'What? Any child knows that! And don't you know Rabbi Nussbaum once demanded that all Germans be castrated?' So, completely mad and fantastic stories. I invented this example, I should add, but the arguments are of that kind. They boast of knowledge that is difficult to verify but which, because they are unverifiable, lend the person who presents them a special form of authority. I think it is therefore wise to be especially vigilant whenever people operate with such seemingly very concrete assertions. This is combined with the famous Hitlerian technique of the bare-faced lie. Thus, at German election rallies, the NPD exaggerated the payments, the compensation payments to Israel, tenfold – and systematically so. But then it came out, and there were energetic demonstrations against it, and they are now having considerable problems because of it.

Something that belongs in the same context is the 'salami method', as some term it with a flippant German expression – that is, cutting off a piece from a complex, then another and then another. So, for example, using the pseudo-scientific pedantry peculiar to these movements, they cast doubt on the number of murdered Jews.

And first they say, 'Well, it wasn't six million, only five and a half', and from that point it soon becomes dubious whether any were murdered at all, and finally things are presented as if it had actually been the other way around. So I think that one should view these matters with particular vigilance.

A further important characteristic of this way of thinking – and this is the complement to concretism, as it were – is formalism. Especially a formalism of the juridical kind. For example, saying that the Munich Agreement was signed voluntarily by the Western powers and is therefore still legally valid, including all the resulting claims – including the Sudetenland, for example, and whatever else.

Then I think I have already said – no, I have not spoken about it yet, it is something that I am not sure applies also to Austria; it definitely applies to Germany, and I could imagine that it is also an immediate concern here. It is what I call the trick of the official or the certified, by which I mean that these groups use nomenclature that suggests they are approved and supported by some official authorities. For example, the most widely read rightist magazine, which is aimed at students, is called *Studenten-Anzeiger*, which creates the impression, to the naive observer, that it is produced by a student organization with the backing of the students, whereas it is actually a purely propagandist affair. Similarly, the word 'German' is monopolized. Every conceivable thing is referred to as 'German', while the opposing parties, simply because they are at home in Germany and operate there, are just as German as those who monopolize the word.

But I would still like to address one trick here, for it is by no means a mere trick but something one seriously encounters time and again. This is the trick of 'One has to have an idea.' It is something one also finds among relatively harmless and merely rather simple people, who say, 'Well, what is to become of our young people? These young people have no idea, and at least they give them an idea.' Now, I spoke to you earlier of vulgar idealism. I think this is really the prototype of what I meant by vulgar idealism, because here the concept of the idea is pragmatically turned into its opposite. That is, the idea is meant to exist not because it is true, not for its objective substance, but only for the pragmatic reason that one allegedly cannot live without an idea, that it is supposed to be good to have an idea. The actual content of the idea does not matter. But if one simply bangs on the table in the right way and says, 'We have an idea', then this is already an effective surrogate for such an idea. So I would say that here, whenever one hears the call 'We must have an idea again', one should also be especially vigilant.

As far as nationalism is concerned, it does not usually appear in a general form in the propaganda but concentrates very skilfully on certain allergic points. For example, the claim that Germans suffer discrimination in the world, to which one must quite simply respond that, after the monstrousness of what happened, it is actually surprising how little resentment has remained, how quickly it was forgotten. Or they speak of denigrating national symbols, something that then leads directly to fits of rage and acts of violence. The autonomy of the symbol in relation to what it represents is another one of these allergic points that should be very precisely analysed. The reason is probably that, in addition to the expressive content of these symbols, there are implicit meanings quite different from the merely national element they supposedly stand for, and that the unconscious reacts to quite different threats when these symbols are allegedly not adequately respected, as this propaganda pretends. There is a similar tendency to brand those people who recognize the Oder–Neisse line[4] as 'traitors to the country'. There have been similar things before – one spoke of 'fulfilment politicians' in the Weimar Republic. This is the complex one could term 'punitiveness' towards others.

Recently a major institution of public communication in Germany had a meeting with a few NPD leaders to find out what concrete suggestions they actually had. And the only concrete suggestion that came out of it – and this is very telling – was that the death sentence for the murderers of taxi drivers should be reintroduced. That is, I think that sounds very laughable and insignificant, but it shows how significant a part a sadism cloaked in legal ideas continues to play in these matters.

I will refrain from analysing in detail some of the other tricks that are typical of the current situation. Such as the phrase, 'So we're not allowed to do what every negro state is allowed to?' – which raises the question of what that actually is. Or the claim that German business has sold out to foreign capital at the same time as there is a lack of capital within German industry. Or the claim of foreign domination through guest workers – when the need for labour power, despite increasing unemployment, is in fact so great in a whole range of professions, the most menial ones, that this need for foreign workers – I prefer 'foreign worker' to 'guest worker', for I consider 'guest worker' an ideological term – this need continues. Then obviously the whole complex of 'degenerate art', 'cleanliness', 'clean canvas' and whatever else is connected to these things.

This area also includes the complex 'enough admissions of guilt', which were never really demanded anyway. Then the claim that National Socialism was initially healthy and then 'got out of hand'. Generally the doctrine of the healthy core. Then the claim of tallying up guilt. And finally the polemic against the Nazi trials; Fritz Bauer once observed quite correctly that the same people who insist on reintroducing the death penalty demand that the murderers of Auschwitz go unpunished, something one should definitely point out in this context, though I will not deny that there is a very serious contradiction here, a contradiction I have racked my brains to address theoretically.

Now, let me say just a few more words about the matter of resistance. I think the 'hush hush' tactic – that is, the tactic of keeping quiet about these things – has never paid off, and this development has surely advanced much too far today for it to work. I have already told you that one should appeal to the real interests instead of moralizing; I can only repeat it once more. Perhaps I can also remind you of one of the findings from our *Authoritarian Personality* research in America, which revealed that even prejudiced personalities, who were certainly authoritarian, repressive, politically and economically reactionary, when it came to their own transparent interests, transparent to themselves, reacted quite differently. So they were mortal enemies of the Roosevelt administration, for example, but with those institutions that were of direct benefit to them, such as tenant protection or cheaper medicines, that was where their anti-Rooseveltianism immediately stopped and they behaved relatively rationally. This split in people's consciousness strikes me as one of the most promising points of departure to counter the developments I have discussed.

A further aspect is the turn inwards. What I mean is that, in opposing these movements, one tries to convey that the substance of this entire complex of authority-bound personality and extreme right-wing ideology is not, in reality, the designated enemy, not about the people they rage against; rather, it is about elements of projection. That is, the real subjects of a study that would need to be understood and changed are the right-wing extremists, not those against whom they mobilize their hatred. Now, ladies and gentlemen, I am not so naive as to think that one can achieve a great deal with the people in question simply through this turn inwards, for it is a substantial part – there is no more time for me to explain in detail why that is – it is a substantial part of this syndrome that these authority-bound characters are inaccessible, that they will not let anything get through to them. Nonetheless – and I must ask you to forgive me if I refer to *The Authoritarian Personality* once again – nonetheless it transpired that, simply by making a socio-psychological problem out of these personalities who behave in this way and not any other, by reflecting on them, and on the connections between their ideology and their psychological, their socio-psychological structures, by making this a problem, a certain naivety in the social climate has been eliminated and a certain detoxification has taken place. And I could imagine that this might be a promising approach in the various German-speaking countries too.

Finally, one should identify the tricks I have spoken of, give them very drastic names, describe them precisely, describe their implications and thus attempt to immunize the masses against these tricks, as it were, for nobody wants to be the fool – or, as they would say in Vienna, nobody wants to be the *Wurzen*. And it can certainly be shown that the entire thing is based on a gigantic psychological *Wurztechnik*, a gigantic psychological rip-off.

Now, ladies and gentlemen, I repeat that I am aware that right-wing extremism is not a psychological and ideological problem but a very real and political one. Yet the factually wrong, untrue nature of its own substance forces it to operate with ideological means, which in this case take the form of propagandist means. And that is why, aside from the political struggle by purely political means, one must confront it on its very own turf. But we must not fight lies with lies, we must not try to be just as clever as it is, but we must counteract it with the full force of reason, with the genuinely unideological truth.

Perhaps some of you will ask me, or would like to ask me, what I think about the future of right-wing extremism. I think this is the wrong question, for it is much too contemplative. This way of thinking, which views such things from the outset like natural disasters about which one makes predictions, like whirlwinds or meteorological disasters, this already shows a form of resignation whereby one essentially eliminates oneself as a political subject; it expresses a harmfully spectator-like relationship with reality. How these things will continue, and the responsibility for how they will continue, that ultimately lies in our hands. Thank you for listening.

Publisher's Note

Theodor W. Adorno gave his lecture on 'Aspects of the New Right-Wing Extremism' on 6 April 1967 on the invitation of the Austrian Socialist Students' Association at the new department building of the University of Vienna. Adorno used seven pages of hand-written notes and key-words; these have survived in his literary estate. The present edition is based on the tape record-ing, which was also taken up into the Austrian Media Library. The text is a pre-publication from the volume *Vorträge 1949–1968*, edited by Michael Schwarz for Suhrkamp Verlag, which will appear in the series of Adorno's posthumous writings under the overall editorship of the Theodor W. Adorno Archive.

Afterword by Volker Weiss

Theodor W. Adorno's deliberations on 'Aspects of the New Right-Wing Extremism' from 1967 constitute one of the philosopher's public interventions. As a purely spoken lecture at the University of Vienna, previously existing only as a tape recording, it has remained virtually unknown. More than half a century later, however, one is struck by the continued validity of his analysis, which reads in parts like a commentary on current developments.

Adorno was ambivalent towards recordings and transcriptions, as is known from the editorial history of other lectures he gave. To him, the reproduction of the freely spoken word blurred its fundamental difference from writing. He considered such reproductions part of 'the behaviours of the administered world, which even pins down the ephemeral word, whose truth lies in its own transience, to place the speaker under oath.'[1] In contrast to the ephemeral form of oral presentation, however, the content of this lecture is anything but fleeting in nature and justifies the publication of what was spoken back then.

The Vienna speech can be read as a continuation of the 1959 lecture 'The Meaning of Working through the Past'.[2] For all its current relevance, then, it has a solid place in Adorno's output. His deliberately loose reflections served to explain to an Austrian audience the rise of the German NPD, founded in 1964, which was gaining significant popularity as a collective movement on the right. By 1968 it would gain seats in the regional parliaments of seven German states. The narrow defeat of the NPD in the 1969 general election was not yet foreseeable at the time of the lecture. Because of the concrete topic, Adorno made his more fundamental reflections on the historical and social conditions of this development rather cursory. He gave more attention to the socio-psychological dispositions of the Germans and the ways in which fascist agitation functions.

Speaking in 1967, it was obvious that Adorno would invoke the historical experience of National Socialism as a reference point. The publication of the spoken text now augments the two stages of his reflections with a third. In addition to his historical vanishing point, National Socialism, and the immediate context of the speech, namely the 1960s, there is now a present in which an extreme right is once again emerging as an influential political force. This lends Adorno's words their relevance; yet one should avoid any simplistic equivalence. In his lecture, Adorno himself emphasizes the differences between his time and the Weimar period. Likewise, analogies to National Socialism were tenable only to an extent. The same applies to comparing the present day in 2019 to the time fifty years ago. Reading the speech thus requires that we distinguish between context-dependent and fundamental aspects. Its far-sighted relevance must be seen in relation to its temporal, historical core.

At times these two levels merge, for Adorno was speaking in Vienna not only as a critical analyst of the situation, but also as a witness of the time. He had experienced how willingly the bourgeois elites had supported National Socialism – directly on 3 April 1933, when the University of Frankfurt ended its association with the Institute of Social Research (ISR). Max Horkheimer was dismissed immediately, along with other staff considered undesirable either 'racially' or in their worldview. No one, in Rolf Wiggershaus's description of the events, intervened to defend 'their ostracized and persecuted colleagues'.[3] With the return of the ISR to the old world after the war, circumstances in Germany approached the situation discussed in the lecture.

This decision to move the institute back to Frankfurt was by no means an automatic one. Europe, as the outcome of the war had shown, was the past. The staff at the ISR knew that the future of Western society, and thus their object of analysis, would henceforth be decided in the USA. The American model based on capitalism and democracy expedited the development of serial production, mass consumption and the culture industry – those fields that were central to their theory of society. Tendencies that would shape Europe were anticipated there. Adorno saw this as the manifestation of a historical tendency.[4] This interpretation discerned a historical development without equating the two models. The difference lay especially, though not exclusively, in the Holocaust, which was more a product of National Socialism than of Fordism.

But the ISR had never lost sight of Germany or National Socialism. A lecture series at Columbia University in the spring of 1945, entitled 'The Repercussions of National Socialism', testified to the contradictory situation. On the one hand, the lectures proved how intensively the institute was continuing its analysis of Germany and Europe. On the other hand, it 'clearly suggested that the crucial problems of Germany and Europe were best studied from the USA.'[5] Consistently with this, the institute had based its large-scale project *Studies in Prejudice* on data from the USA. Nonetheless, in 1949, the inner circle of the institute – Horkheimer, Adorno and Friedrich Pollock – made the decision to return. The step was also motivated by a paradoxical hope that, in Germany's less developed society, rudiments of a time before total socialization, residues of educational ideals and bourgeois subjectivity – in short, European culture – would have stayed alive, having vanished in the fast-moving USA.

Finding the framework for a new beginning in Frankfurt was no easy matter. Horkheimer described in 1948 how, at exploratory talks, the university officials greeted him in a 'sweet, slick and insincerely honourable' way: 'They don't know yet whether to see me as a relatively influential traveller of America or as the brother of their victims, whose intention is remembrance. They have to decide on the latter.'[6] But soon after the war, as in the USA, the political direction of the occupying authorities in West Germany had also shifted from anti-fascism to anti-communism. The new line was oriented towards ensuring German loyalty in the incipient East–West conflict. This increased the resonance echo of National Socialism in society, and the institute's work focused on this.

A group experiment was initiated in 1950, on the model of the *Studies*, to assess the attitudes of young Germans to the Nazi dictatorship and the occupation, to guilt and democracy, using new empirical methods developed in the USA. The result described a demoscopic phenomenon that is known to this day: a 'non-public opinion ... whose content can deviate very considerably from the content of the public opinion, but whose formulations circulate alongside those of the public opinion like monetary units of a second currency.'[7] This showed that the convention of civilizatory-democratic chastening was scarcely capable of keeping the latency of fascist elements under control. Any weakness in the higher authority and the appropriate stimuli were enough to let it come rapidly to the surface again, a pattern reminiscent of processes familiar from psychoanalysis. The findings showed early on that fascism does not require any party to survive, and that a party can quickly be formed by falling back on such 'non-public' resentments.

This was not welcome news. In the light of the findings of the group experiment, opponents of the institute resorted to a 'tried and tested procedure which is popular to this day: playing down the dangers from the right, presenting the "exposers" of such dangers as totalitarian moralists and idealists'.[8] Today, by contrast, the pioneering work of the ISR is as undisputed as its significance for current studies: 'The significant discussions about right-wing populism are based on questions that could only be asked using the conceptual apparatus derived from the institute's studies on prejudice', namely what 'psychological advantage' was gained through denigrations, why 'one's own (genuine or pretextual) fear' acted as a justification for resentments, and how 'racism, anti-Semitism and sexism', as well as 'the nation-state, capitalism and racism, are connected.'[9] The ISR and Adorno himself had spent decades working on such complexes. In the light of this, his declaration in Vienna that he simply wanted to add to a few thoughts was a remarkable understatement.

At the moment of his lecture, then, Adorno was speaking from the experience gained through emigration and research, as well as everyday life in a country where, a little over two decades earlier, right-wing extremism had been state doctrine. The central idea of his speech is a variation on the oft-quoted warning, already formulated in 1959, that 'the survival of National Socialism in democracy' is 'more threatening than the survival of fascist tendencies against democracy'. It is precisely the latter that were now becoming visible in political events. While Adorno had said eight years earlier that he did 'not wish to go into the question of neo-Nazi organizations', it had now become necessary to pay attention to this phenomenon.[10]

In 'Aspects of the New Right-Wing Extremism', Adorno speaks – as before – of

49

'pathic' nationalism and discusses the *tricks* of the propaganda as well as the traces of narcissistic injury in society as a result of defeat.[11] Even reflections on appeals to rational interest and the *full force of reason* are developed once again. Through this reuse of terms, it is not hard to recognize the 'planks' of the fascist 'platform' that he and Horkheimer had already outlined in the *Dialectic of Enlightenment*.[12] The repeated reference to the structure of the *authority-bound personality* is drawn from the study of the same name conducted as part of the institute's research on prejudice. Overall, the lecture evokes several familiar motifs from the institute's research, which already saw the transition from Weimar democracy to National Socialism 'not as a rupture, but as a quasi-logical evolution'.[13] Even after 1945, the structural contradiction between democratic participation and the *tendency towards concentration of capital*, which was at the centre of analysis at the time, was not resolved. *In that sense*, Adorno says, *one might refer to the fascist movements as the wounds, the scars of a democracy that, to this day, has not yet lived up to its own concept.*

Despite all reservations about historical comparisons, Adorno's examples thus testify to the longevity of individual fields of conflict. Regional continuities in electoral behaviour strike him as the *ghost of a ghost*, and this revenant still haunts some places today.[14] The failure of the less radical forces in the NPD during the 1960s reminded Adorno of the part played by the German Nationalists in the rise of the Nazi Party; this pattern continues today in the failure of efforts to tame extremists. The comments on the antagonistic character of nationalism and its resurgence as an *attempt to assert oneself in the midst of integration* read like a description of the current disengagements within the EU, exemplified by the Brexit debates in the UK and the Vote Leave campaign's slogan 'Take back control'. The development of resentment still revolves around the question of 'how much control one feels one has over one's own life'.[15] Adorno recognized this significance of emotions decades before the revolt of the so-called angry citizens [*Wutbürger*] – a development that refutes the belief that the introduction of the EU's single market had done away once and for all with a nationalism based on fears of decline. Today too, the call for sovereignty, which already had *something fictitious* about it back then on account of the complex systems of reference in modernity, can become one of the main slogans of right-wing anti-Europeans.

In its analysis of the connection between economy, society and subject structure, critical theory operates on a terrain entirely its own. Adorno's remark on *technological unemployment* as a consequence of automation can therefore remain succinct, as it takes up a long discussion on the relationship between the constitution of the subject and technological development in capitalism. Already in 1941, Herbert Marcuse had, in some notes 'on the social consequences of modern technology', and explicitly with reference to the 'technocratic' character of National Socialism, retraced the decline of the bourgeois subject to a pure carrier of efficiency and performance.[16]

Two years earlier, Max Horkheimer had described how 'the extremely technologically advanced industry' undermined the principle of liberalism, as its development 'makes the sale of labour power impossible for large sections of the populace'.[17] The tendency towards crisis is structural and generates a *feeling of social catastrophe* as a *distortion of Marx's theory of collapse* that extends into the middle classes. This feeling caused something to shift in the subjects, for now they await the emergency, or even long for it. Adorno thus sees the contemporary economic crisis *anticipated* in the political one preceding it, namely the rise of the NPD. The endpoint is not the striving for change but an escape to gleeful apocalyptic rhetoric. *Do you know what Wotan wants? The end.*

The knowledge that one could be more, but is not, still drives people to acts of collective narcissism. Stefan Breuer summarizes this phenomenon, which already featured in Adorno's lecture 'The Meaning of Working through the Past':

> In making the collective subject of the nation or the leader into their ideal and ascribing fantastic properties to it, individuals achieve part of that archaic oversized self whose realization is impossible in the existence of each on their own; at the same time, they liberate themselves through projection from their own aggressions that are tied to the ego-ideal, with the inevitable consequence that the world is peopled by dangerous, vengeful objects against which the subject must in turn defend itself: the drawback of the gratifications that 'socialized narcissism' provides is paranoia.[18]

This pattern continues to be effective. The experience of being interchangeable as an employee can thus lead to the rightist phantasm of a 'great replacement' between ethnic groups.[19] Seeking help, concerned individuals turn to an imagined sovereign. They see an authoritarian nation-state no longer as a threat but as a protection and an incarnation of what is their 'own' – a process that had led Horkheimer to remark already in the 1930s that, in late capitalism, peoples changed 'first into recipients of support, then into followings'.[20] Instead of being swallowed up by an administered world, they prefer to choose a directly palpable authority.

What is the value of these analyses for the present day? One must first of all note the differences. Adorno's warning of a simplistic attribution of right-wing extremism to economic movements should be taken seriously. The effects of the 1966–7 recession as the immediate background to the developments described are comparable neither to the consequences of the 1929 global economic crisis nor to those of current financial and monetary crises. Adorno's scepticism towards an exaggeration of activities among former Nazi Party members was likewise correct. In fact, there was a generational shift in the late 1960s that marked a transition from an old to a new right. A fundamental aspect of this was a substantial adaptation among the most extreme rightists after 1945, the removal, as Adorno says, of *openly anti-democratic aspects*. They were replaced by a new self-representation whose description by Adorno also characterizes the right-wing populists of today: *they constantly invoke true democracy and accuse the others of being anti-democratic.*

Today, the pressure to conform described by Adorno is greatly attenuated via the culture industry. In the shadow of the commodity fetish there are numerous possibilities for an individualized conformity whose effects extend to the leadership of the current right; its charisma offers barely more than a caricature of the past. Nor are the political frontlines directly comparable. The confrontation with global jihad, a key element in the incitement by right-wing populists, is – unlike anti-Semitism – not purely a matter of pathic projection. Political Islam is a genuine actor and must itself be understood as the product of a collective narcissistic injury. By being willing to engage with this area too in future, critical theory can show its ability 'to react to current and concrete threats'.[21]

The ISR examined how fascism was able to rise together with Fordism. The question today is, what did the remnants of bourgeois subjectivity turn into in the subsequent period? Digitization pushed the *automation* mentioned by Adorno even further. In the age of hi-tech, forcing human labour into precarious areas again caused feelings of injury. Against the background of the decline of the political left, Didier Eribon rightly asks who really 'takes into account' that the superfluous, the precariously employed and the leftovers of the industrial proletariat exist, 'how they live, what they think about, what they want'.[22]

These aspects point to a large gap in the debate about the current authoritarian revolt, which is not based solely on racism. Rather, it incorporates resentments that can be extended to such groups as socialists and liberals. Those who are threatened by decline often lay the blame for their misery *not on the apparatus that causes it, but on those who were critical towards the system in which they once had a status.*

All those who suggest different models become a particular object of anger, as shown by the current fixation of the extreme right on a left that has been largely powerless for decades. The bugbear of a quasi-dictatorial 'left-green-infested, 1968-generation Germany'[23] shows that traditional bogeymen can still spread terror under completely different social conditions. Abandoning all categories, the European Union is referred to as the 'EUSSR', Germany as 'GDR 2.0' and the Affordable Care Act ('Obamacare') as 'socialist', while the entire political landscape, even large areas of democratic conservatism, are classified as 'left'. Communism, already more *imago* than concept in 1967, and thus *divorced from any knowledge about the matter*, can still be effectively invoked.

The discourse continues to be marked by the intersection of anti-intellectualism, anti-Marxism and anti-Semitism, Adorno's *bête noire*, which was already described in the chapter on anti-Semitism from the *Dialectic of Enlightenment*. It has once again become rampant in the figure of so-called cultural Marxism. This term, taken from the most extreme sector of the US right, has meanwhile taken over from the Nazi propaganda phrase 'cultural Bolshevism'. It is common all over the world and constructs a conspiracy theory with critical theory itself, notably, at the centre.[24]

Powerful verbal attacks are also directed at a historical processing of the National Socialist past inspired by Adorno. Trembling with pathos, a leading AfD[25] politician announced it was time to end an 'idiotic politics of dealing with the past' and demanded a 'U-turn in our remembrance politics'.[26] This rhetoric had already been used by the NPD; Adorno summarizes it as *the complex 'enough admissions of guilt'*. This recourse to the past, something in which present-day right-wing populists in Germany are no different from other right-wing parties of recent decades, confirms how precisely Adorno had already grasped the motives of those demanding an end to the 'cult of guilt'.[27] The injury caused by the knowledge of the atrocities committed by one's own nation is turned against those who urge remembrance and against remembrance itself. As early as 1959, Adorno recognized that one element of 'forgetting what has barely transpired' was the 'fury of one who must first talk himself out of what everyone knows, before he can then talk others out of it as well.'[28] In his observation of these affects, Adorno is speaking as the same returned 'brother' of the victims already feared by the Frankfurt officials in the guise of the returned Horkheimer.

Even today, as in Adorno's time, *the mention of Auschwitz* is as likely to send people *into a rage* as general ethical considerations or *appeals to humanity*, something expressed in talk of 'do-gooders' or the calls of 'Let 'em drown' directed at sea rescuers at a Pegida rally in 2018. Right-wing agitators are now going even further, however, by regularly equating themselves with the victims.[29]

Many of these affects seem like relics of another time, but their anachronism is precisely what makes them effective. When the promises of a prosperous present prove deceptive, when personal status is under threat, then identity becomes a fetish and tendencies return that had been thought overcome. As Adorno notes, *convictions and ideologies take on their demonic, their genuinely destructive character precisely when the objective situation has deprived them of substance.* Today the immense pull of misogynistic and homophobic agitation in times of equal rights or the revival of religious fundamentalism in the midst of a secular present show how deceptive a sense of security in the light of civilizational advances can be. Eribon is amazed how energetically 'certain categories of the population – gay men, lesbians, transsexuals, Jews, blacks, and so on – have to bear the burden of these social and cultural curses'.[30] As one might say with recourse to the *Dialectic of Enlightenment*, they are begrudged the purely abstract right to liberate themselves by those who can understand happiness only as an expression of concrete power.[31]

Adorno's observation that *in these extreme right-wing movements, propaganda actually constitutes the substance of politics* is still absolutely valid. Here he follows on seamlessly from Leo Löwenthal's *False Prophets*, whose analysis of fascist agitation in the USA, another study belonging to the large-scale *Prejudice* project, highlights how fundamental an invocation of emergency is in propaganda.[32] Löwenthal's findings are already sufficient to crush the hope that the extreme right would moderate itself as soon as it grew used to certain discursive rules or was politically integrated. Löwenthal describes the systematic stimulation of the authoritarian personality as 'turning psychoanalysis on its head'. He argues that what applies to 'mass culture' in general also applies to the technique of agitation: 'It makes people neurotic and psychotic and finally completely dependent on their so-called leaders.'[33]

Adorno had already presented Löwenthal's findings in 1944 at a symposium held by the psychoanalyst Ernst Simmel.[34] He knew that the political destruction produced by the right-wing demagogues resulted not from uncontrolled outbursts that could be curbed but actually from pure calculation. For him it was beyond doubt that 'fascist propaganda, with all its twisted logic and fantastic distortions, is consciously planned and organized.' Yet it 'does not employ discursive logic but is rather ... what might be called an organized flight of ideas.'[35] This makes appeals to the agitator's reason futile. Adorno's later sigh that *one must truly be stricken with the spirit of formalism not to see what they mean* can be directly transferred to offers of discussion today.

The effect of agitation is also guaranteed by the framework of the culture industry, which it resembles down to its details. In the Internet age, the combination Adorno notes between an *extraordinary perfection of certain methods* and a *complete abstruseness of the aims* emerges all the more clearly. Their manifestations as bots, trolls and fake news have received much attention.

Beneath this surface, what becomes visible is precisely the *constellation of rational means and irrational ends* that Adorno also identifies as an *overall tendency of civilization* beyond such excesses. It is still the case that fighting propaganda is a futile endeavour without reflection on the mechanisms of mass-produced information and culture, as this framework is what allows propaganda to take effect in the first place. In the light of this structure, discreet silence or downplaying, the *hush hush tactic*, is equally ineffective.

This recalls Löwenthal's objection to Walter Benjamin's reflections on mass culture, namely that Benjamin's optimism that 'the dissemination of works of art made possible by mechanical and electronic means of reproduction can also have a positive political effect' in fact 'ran counter to all our experiences' at the institute.[36] Today the digital revolution has not only taken mass culture to a new level but also provided the state and business with further instruments to expand the complete administration of society. Like their historical forerunners, the leaders of the contemporary extreme right are virtuosos in combining propaganda and technology. The successful employment of these means at the 2016 presidential election in the USA serves as a model for rightist movements in Europe, which have been veritably Americanized since then in both style and content. The transatlantic perspective adopted by the ISR continues to be valid.

After almost three decades of digital communication, it is evident that the hope of a technologically mediated boost in democracy cannot be fulfilled as long as the culture industry's framework of kitsch and spectacle remains dominant. This problem also arises in activities against the rising extreme right if they rely on the same patterns: simply defending the status quo will fail as a defensive strategy without the realization that the rightist renaissance is itself a result of that same status quo. Adorno – and Löwenthal – already saw this connection over half a century ago.

So there is no reason to historicize critical theory. At present the political centre is becoming less wary of the far right, and parts of middle-class society are returning to the constellation they abandoned in the liberal post-war decades. They are once more applauding a fascist agitator who demands 'that the rupture must grow even deeper, that our language must become even clearer, even more concrete'.[37] The synthesis of the educated elite and liberal democracy that has defined the intellectual landscape of many Western countries since the 1960s is not nature-given; it can end.

In these days too, the ghost with which Adorno's lecture deals is far from being put to rest; it is haunting society again as the *new right-wing extremism*. This makes it all the more important to regain an awareness of the structure of fascist agitation, as well as the socio-psychological foundations of its success. The work done by Adorno and the Institute of Social Research is an indispensable part of this.

About the Authors

Theodor W. Adorno (1903–1969) was a philosopher and sociologist. He was one of the main exponents of critical theory as practised by the Frankfurt School, which emerged from the Institute of Social Research at the University of Frankfurt. In addition, with his lectures, radio broadcasts and publications, he had a formative influence on cultural and intellectual life in post-war Germany.

Volker Weiss, born in 1972, is a historian and publicist. His research includes studies on the historical and contemporary extreme right. His book *The Authoritarian Revolt: The New Right and the Decline of the West* is considered one of the standard works on the New Right.

Notes

Aspects of the New Right-Wing Extremism

1 A collective movement that initially united a spectrum extending from national conservatives to right-wing extremists and, as a party, became the leading German neo-Nazi organization. In the new millennium it became largely insignificant.

2 The word translated here as 'choose', *wählen*, also means 'to vote', which makes the statement ambiguous (Trans.).

3 In his lecture 'On the Problem of Social Conflict Today'.

4 The border between Germany and Poland (Trans.).

Afterword

1 Theodor W. Adorno, 'Zur Bekämpfung des Antisemitismus heute', *Das Argument* 6/29 (1964), p. 88.

Also in Adorno, *Gesammelte Schriften* [*GS*], ed. Rolf Tiedemann (Frankfurt am Main: Suhrkamp, 1997), vol. 20: *Vermischte Schriften*, p. 360.

2 Adorno, 'The Meaning of Working through the Past', in *Critical Models: Interventions and Catchwords*, trans. Henry W. Pickford (New York: Columbia University Press, 2005), pp. 89–104.

3 Rolf Wiggershaus, *The Frankfurt School: Its History, Theories, and Political Significance*, trans. Michael Robertson (Cambridge, MA: MIT Press, 1994), p. 129.

4 When Germany capitulated, Adorno wrote to Horkheimer that 'the war was won by industry against the military, in keeping with the overall tendency of history.' Letter from 9 May 1945, in Theodor W. Adorno and Max Horkheimer, *Briefwechsel 1927–1969*, ed. Christoph Gödde and Henri Lonitz, vol. 3: *1945–1949* (Frankfurt am Main: Suhrkamp, 2005), p. 101.

5 Wiggershaus, *The Frankfurt School*, p. 385.

6 Letter from Max Horkheimer to Maidon Horkheimer from 26 May 1948, in Max Horkheimer, *Gesammelte Schriften*, ed. Alfred Schmidt and Gunzelin Schmid Noerr, vol. 17: *Briefwechsel 1941–1948* (Frankfurt am Main: Suhrkamp, 1996), p. 976.

7 *Frankfurter Beiträge zur Soziologie*, vol. 2: *Gruppenexperiment: Ein Studienbericht*, ed. Friedrich Pollock with a foreword by Franz Böhm (Frankfurt am Main: Campus, 1955), p. xi.

8   Wiggershaus, *The Frankfurt School*, p. 477.
9   Marc Grimm, 'Zur Aktualität Kritischer Theorie', *Zeitschrift für Politische Theorie* 8/1 (2017), p. 116.
10 Adorno, 'The Meaning of Working through the Past', p. 90.
11 The italicized terms, phrases and passages are direct quotations from Adorno's lecture in this volume.
12 Max Horkheimer and Theodor W. Adorno, *Dialectic of Enlightenment*, trans. Edmund Jephcott (Stanford, CA: Stanford University Press, 2002), p. 172.
13 Helmut Dubiel and Alfons Söllner, 'Die Nationalsozialismusforschung des Instituts für Sozialforschung – ihre wissenschaftliche Stellung und gegenwärtige Bedeutung', in *Horkheimer, Pollock, Neumann, Kirchheimer, Gurland, Marcuse: Wirtschaft, Recht und Staat im Nationalsozialismus: Analysen des Instituts für Sozialforschung 1939–1942* (Frankfurt am Main: Europäische Verlags-Anstalt, 1981), p. 9.
14 See Davide Cantoni, Felix Hagemeister and Mark Westcott, *Persistence and Activation of Right-Wing Political Ideology* (2019), https://rationality-and-competition.de/wp-content/uploads/discussion_paper/143.pdf.
15 Uffa Jensen, *Zornpolitik* (Berlin: Suhrkamp, 2017), p. 38.
16 Herbert Marcuse, 'Einige gesellschaftliche Folgen moderner Technologie', in Dubiel and Söllner

(eds), *Horkheimer, Pollock, Neumann, Kirchheimer, Gurland, Marcuse*, p. 341.

[17] Max Horkheimer, 'Die Juden und Europa', ibid., p. 34.

[18] Stefan Breuer, 'Adornos Anthropologie', *Leviathan* 12/3 (1984), pp. 346f.

[19] See Renaud Camus, *Le Grand Remplacement* (Paris: David Reinharc, 2011). The notion of the 'great replacement' is among the central propaganda phrases of the New Right. The manifesto published by the perpetrator of the 2019 Christchurch massacre was likewise entitled 'The Great Replacement'.

[20] Horkheimer, 'Die Juden und Europa', p. 37.

[21] Grimm, 'Zur Aktualität Kritischer Theorie', p. 120.

[22] Didier Eribon, *Returning to Reims*, trans. Michael Lucey (Los Angeles: Semiotext(e), 2013), p. 46.

[23] Jörg Meuthen at the party conference of the AfD [see note 25 below] in Stuttgart in 2016.

[24] See Alice Weidel, 'Die Angst der Kulturmarxistenvor der Aufklärung und der AfD', *JungeFreiheit*, 23 May 2018, https://jungefreiheit.de/debatte/kommentar/2018/die-angst-der-kulturmarxisten-vor-der-aufklaerung-und-der-afd. The term 'cultural Marxism' also plays a central part in the manifesto '2083'by the Norwegian mass murderer Anders Breivik from 2011. Breivik was inspired in his worldview by the Norwegian blogger 'Fjordman', whose texts likewise propagate a battle against 'cultural Marxism'. A selection was translated into German after Breivik's

massacre, and another had previously been published in English as *Defeating Eurabia* (Morrisville, NC: Lulu, 2008). Robert Bowers, who was charged with murdering eight people in 2018 at the Tree of Life Synagogue in Pittsburgh, likewise saw himself as a soldier in the war on cultural Marxism. See Samuel Moyn, 'The Alt-Right's Favourite Meme is 100 Years Old', *New York Times*, 12 November 2018, www.nytimes.com/2018/11/13/opinion/cultural-marxism-anti-semitism.html.

25 Alternative für Deutschland [Alternative for Germany] was founded in 2013 as a right-wing populist party that made a name for itself primarily through its criticism of European monetary policy. After a change of leadership in 2015, it came under the control of extreme right-wing cadres and changed its main issue from monetary policy to immigration. It received 12.6 per cent of votes at the general election in 2017 and is now represented in all sixteen state parliaments.

26 Björn Höcke in a speech on 17 January 2017 at the Dresden restaurant Ballhaus Watzke.

27 'A hundred years after the birth of the "ugly German" from the spirit of British war propaganda, it is surely time gradually to discard the cult of guilt and our national neuroses. The unpleasant side of the "typically German" is now a pride in guilt, a pleasure in pillorying oneself when others have long adopted a more nuanced view.' Michael Paulwitz,

'Der Selbsthass blüht', *Junge Freiheit*, 23 May 2014, p. 13.

28 Adorno, 'The Meaning of Working through the Past', p. 92.

29 'The people who live in Germany have grown used to coping with anti-Germanism, just as Jews had to learn to deal with anti-Semitism.' Rolf Peter Sieferle, *Finis Germania* (Schnellroda: Antaios, 2017), p. 77.

30 Eribon, *Returning to Reims*, p. 217.

31 Horkheimer and Adorno, *Dialectic of Enlightenment*, p. 142.

32 Leo Löwenthal, *False Prophets: Studies on Authoritarianism* (New Brunswick, NJ: Transaction, 1987).

33 Leo Löwenthal, 'Scholarly Biography: A Conversation with Helmut Dubiel, 1979', in *Critical Theory and Frankfurt Theorists: Lectures–Correspondence–Conversations* (London: Routledge, 1989), p. 258.

34 Adorno, 'Anti-Semitism and Fascist Propaganda', in *GS*, vol. 8, pp. 397–407. It contains this passage: 'Since the entire weight of this propaganda is to promote the means, propaganda itself becomes the ultimate content' (p. 399).

35 Ibid., p. 401.

36 Löwenthal, 'Scholarly Biography', p. 249.

37 Götz Kubitschek in a discussion between Durs Grünbein and Uwe Tellkamp at the Dresden Kulturpalast on 8 March 2018. How permeable the boundaries have become is also demonstrated by the fact that Uwe Tellkamp has published in

Kubitschek's magazine *Sezession*: Uwe Tellkamp, 'Der Moralismus der Vielen: Offener Brief', *Sezession* 87 (2018), pp. 27–31. It first appeared online on 13 November 2018 (https://sezession.de/59871/der-moralismus-der-vielen-ein-offener-brief-von-uwe-tellkamp).